Career Quest

EXPLORING HEALTH-CARE CAREERS

KELLEY BARTH

TWENTY-FIRST CENTURY BOOKS / MINNEAPOLIS

For Caitlin and Susie, my favorite nurses

Twenty-First Century Books™
An imprint of Lerner Publishing Group, Inc.
241 First Avenue North
Minneapolis, MN 55401 USA

For reading levels and more information, look up this title at www.lernerbooks.com.

Main body text set in Bembo Std Regular
Typeface provided by Monotype Typography

Library of Congress Cataloging-in-Publication Data

Names: Barth, Kelley author
Title: Exploring health-care careers / Kelley Barth.
Description: Minneapolis : Twenty-First Century Books, [2026] | Series: Career quest | Includes bibliographical references and index. | Audience: Ages 11–18 | Audience: Grades 7–9 | Summary: "From nurses to phlebotomists, health care is a vast, growing field. Explore jobs in the medical professions, including important skill sets, how to prepare for a career, and more"—Provided by publisher.
Identifiers: LCCN 2025011237 (print) | LCCN 2025011238 (ebook) | ISBN 9798765662687 library binding | ISBN 9798348029531 paperback | ISBN 9798765699904 epub
Subjects: LCSH: Medical care—Vocational guidance—Juvenile literature
Classification: LCC R690 .B374 2026 (print) | LCC R690 (ebook) | DDC 610.69—dc23/eng/20250625

LC record available at https://lccn.loc.gov/2025011237
LC ebook record available at https://lccn.loc.gov/2025011238

Manufactured in the United States of America

1 – CG – 12/15/25

CONTENTS

INTRODUCTION

It's early morning in a busy urban hospital. In the emergency room (ER), a team of nurses works to prioritize which patients need assistance most urgently. Down the hallway in the lab, a phlebotomist draws a vial of blood from a patient to send off for testing. Next door, a sonographer begins an ultrasound on a pregnant person. Upstairs in an exam room, a doctor listens carefully to a patient's symptoms to determine the correct diagnosis. Outside the hospital, an emergency medical technician (EMT) drives an ambulance up to the ER doors. In the back of the ambulance, a paramedic gives cardiopulmonary resuscitation (CPR) to a patient.

All around the hospital, health-care workers are busy helping patients. They work fast and collaborate in teams to deliver the best care possible. But it isn't just doctors and nurses caring for patients. The health-care field includes a variety of careers. From doctors to phlebotomists to technologists, these career paths offer an always-changing and important line of work.

This book will explore different career paths in the health-care field. You will learn about these paths and explore ways to pursue them both now and in your future.

Providing friendly and compassionate care can bring a smile to a patient's face.

CHAPTER ONE

Health Care Is Everywhere

The health-care industry is one of the largest occupational fields in the United States. It is a source of millions of jobs and the fastest growing career sector. Health care will continue to be a necessity, and the country will need many compassionate and well-trained individuals to move this field into the future.

Health care can be a demanding field. There are certain traits and skill sets that are important for health-care employees, regardless of what specific career path they choose.

Compassion

While some health-care career paths are more focused in a laboratory or research setting, the vast majority of people in health-care careers work hands-on with patients. Above all, a desire to help people is key in pursuing a health-care career. Health-care providers need to be service-oriented and able to pursue their work with compassion. They need to demonstrate kindness, support, and empathy for the patients

Health care is a collaborative field in which professionals must work as a team.

they work with. When someone requires medical care, it can often be a difficult time for individuals and their families. Many patients are scared, vulnerable, or even in pain. Workers need to show compassion for these challenges and put patients' needs first.

Respect

It is important for health-care providers to respect individual patients' needs, preferences, and cultural beliefs. Every patient is different. Many patients will have different backgrounds and beliefs than their health-care providers. Health-care workers must remember that they don't just treat diseases; they treat individuals.

Part of showing respect to patients is also following the established rules of health care. Certain rules are in place to protect patients, especially regarding their privacy. The Health Insurance Portability and Accountability Act, better known as HIPAA, makes sure that a patient's privacy stays intact. Health-care workers must demonstrate integrity and discretion with patient information. They are not allowed to share information about patients outside of work. This is a very important aspect of a career in the medical field.

Knowledge

Patients want to feel confident that their health-care providers are competent and have the experience and knowledge to advise and treat them correctly. Being detail-oriented is also a helpful skill for workers. Health-care professionals need to pay attention to test results, medical records, personal

Health-care workers must be open to learning new skills, even from their coworkers during a busy shift.

observations, and patient reports. Even the smallest issue could be a solution to the puzzle of helping a patient.

Health-care environments are often fast-paced, and strong problem-solving skills and multitasking often come in handy. Most professionals will face new situations and challenges every day. Being able to make quick decisions and prioritize finding solutions to problems even while busy or under stress are very beneficial skills. If you enjoy challenging yourself and learning new skills, a career in health care may be a good fit for you.

Teamwork and Collaboration in Health Care

Health care is a very collaborative field. Employees need to prioritize teamwork and cooperation.

When choosing a specific career path in the medical field, one thing to consider is what role you prefer to play in a group or on a team. Are you a leader who likes to be in charge and outline the direction of the group? Or do you prefer to work hands-on with a plan that has already been decided and given to you? Many careers in health care have a strict hierarchy of who is in charge and who reports to whom. Do an honest assessment of your strengths and weaknesses when it comes to working in a team. Where do you think you would fit in best? How much responsibility would you prefer to have? How many years of education do you want to undertake?

Utilizing strong teamwork in health care also has an important impact on care overall. As Ted A. James explains in an article for Harvard Medical School, "According to research, team-based care can improve the safety, efficiency, and quality of health care." In health-care settings, each individual plays an equally important role in ensuring that patients experience a helpful, supportive, and safe environment. Each member on a health-care team brings a unique skill set. Using those skill sets and strengths together benefits the entire process.

An important part of teamwork is solid communication. Health-care workers need to prioritize being clear communicators and engaged, active listeners. Listening and prioritizing clear communication are necessary skills to work both with patients and colleagues. It is important to remember that other health-care colleagues aren't the only members on a health-care team. The most important team member is the patient!

Communication and teamwork are especially important when working directly with patients. Health-care workers need to be able to effectively and clearly communicate procedures and medical treatment plans. It is important that patients are able to understand their own health and care plans. It is not the job of the health-care provider to make decisions for patients. Providers need to share all the relevant information and support patients as they make decisions for their own health.

Health-care providers often work together to brainstorm new treatment plans for illnesses or specific patients.

The health-care field is constantly evolving. There is always something new to learn.

A Love of Learning

Health care is always changing and growing. As medical research and technology advance, so do the opportunities to enhance patient care. New techniques and treatments are being developed all the time. Successful health-care workers need to stay up-to-date on current research and medical methods. Changing and improving technology is another important aspect of how the health-care field is always evolving. Over time, medical equipment has become more sophisticated, and treatment plans have become more targeted to individual patients. Even the switch to maintaining medical records electronically has improved the quality of care. People interested in a career in health care need to be open to learning and using new technologies, as much of the equipment they may end up using someday probably isn't even invented yet. A strong sense of curiosity and a love for learning are both skills that will serve you well in the health-care field.

Resilience

The pressures of health care can be intense. Many health-care professionals work long hours. The jobs can be physically and emotionally demanding. This is a line of work where a mistake can potentially have a massive impact on someone else's health and well-being. Health-care workers need to prioritize the health and safety not only of their patients, but also of themselves and their coworkers. They need to pay close attention to their work and keep an eye out to avoid errors. Determination, resilience, and a strong work ethic help keep successful health-care workers motivated even through the challenging times.

Successful health-care workers should also pay attention to areas or processes that can be improved. As mentioned previously, health care is always changing. These changes are an important tool in making health care safer and more effective. People in this line of work should approach their career with a mindset for how they can always help improve and advance the quality of care they are providing.

CHAPTER TWO

Health-Care Careers

The health-care field includes countless different career options. Each career has its own specific focus, demands, educational requirements, responsibilities, and work environment. Investigating different career options is a great way to start thinking about what path may be the best fit for your own interests and skills.

If you are interested in a health-care career but aren't certain about what specific pathway is right for you, think about the specifics of each career. How many years of education do you want to pursue after high school? What kind of work environment and schedule do you want? Do you want to work with a specific population such as children, people with disabilities, or elder adults? Do you prefer doing research or working hands-on with technology and equipment? Do you like having a wide variety of tasks in your day-to-day schedule, or do you prefer to specialize in one area or skill? Whatever your interests and preferences, there is probably a health-care career out there that is right for you.

Physicians

A career as a physician, or doctor, is one of the best-known career options in the health-care field. Physicians can specialize in a variety of areas based on their medical interests. Some physicians focus on primary and preventative care for patients. Some of these primary-care specialties include family medicine physicians, who focus on general health maintenance and treat everyday conditions; pediatricians, who focus on care for children and young adults; and obstetricians and gynecologists (OB/GYNs), who focus on female reproductive health.

Physicians are typically the leaders and decision-makers of a team in a hospital setting and must think and act quickly on behalf of patients.

Keeping meticulous patient records is an important part of most health-care careers. A patient's history can help providers make the right decisions in future situations.

Primary care physicians often establish long-term relationships with their patients and treat them over a span of years. Other types of physicians provide more specialized services and treatment. For example, oncologists diagnose and treat cancer, cardiologists address heart conditions, and psychiatrists focus on mental health. Some physicians also have additional training in performing surgery. Surgeons also have different specialties based on which part of the body they treat. Orthopedic surgeons, for example, treat and perform surgery on bones, muscles, ligaments, and tendons. These examples are just a small number of the potential areas that doctors can specialize in.

Regardless of specialty, all doctors need to complete a bachelor's degree and an advanced medical degree. Each of these degrees typically takes four years to complete. Doctors can pursue two different medical degrees: a doctor of medicine degree or a doctor of osteopathic medicine degree. These degree pathways are similar, but a doctor of osteopathic medicine degree provides additional training in manual manipulations of joints and muscles. This pathway tends to approach medicine from a more holistic perspective.

Physicians also must complete a residency program while they continue to learn and develop their skills in practice. Depending on the specialty, this can take between three and nine additional years. Some physicians pursue additional training or fellowships with a specific focus too. A physician's specialty also influences their salary range. Typically, physicians make at least $240,000 a year or more.

Physician Assistants and Nurse Practitioners

Physician assistants (PAs) and nurse practitioners (NPs) examine and treat patients, typically under the supervision of a physician. It is common to see a PA or an NP instead of a physician, especially in a primary care setting. While there are some differences in the scope of care and training between a PA and an NP, they often serve similar functions. Physician assistants need to have a master's degree, which is typically two years beyond a bachelor's degree. Nurse practitioners, on the other hand, need at least a master's degree, and some go on to pursue a doctorate degree. All nurse practitioner students must first have gone through the schooling and testing requirements to be licensed registered nurses (RNs). On average, both professions make approximately $130,000 a year.

Nursing Careers

A variety of nursing professions are available. Nurses play an important role on health-care teams, helping assess and care for patients. They are often able to spend more hands-on time with patients than physicians can. They are frequently in charge of observing and recording patient symptoms and histories, as well as administering medications. Nurses also help monitor medical equipment and perform diagnostic tests, especially with specialty training. Nurses often specialize in specific health-care departments such as geriatrics, neurology, or emergency care.

Registered and Licensed Practical Nurses

Registered nurses have multiple educational pathway options. Some RNs obtain a four-year bachelor's degree. Other RNs complete a two-year intensive nursing degree. All RNs need to pass a certification test to work in the field. RNs make an average of $86,000 a year.

Licensed practical nurses (LPNs) do similar nursing work, typically under the supervision of an RN. LPNs need to complete a one-year educational program and complete an exam to become licensed to work. LPNs make an average of $60,000 a year.

Nursing Assistants and Orderlies

Nursing assistants, sometimes called aides, work under the supervision of an RN or LPN. Nursing assistants are in charge of helping patients with their basic needs and daily care. They help patients with bathing, dressing, eating, and personal hygiene. They also measure basic vital signs such as temperature and blood pressure. The educational and certification requirements for nursing assistants vary by state. Typically, they must complete a short educational program and pass a certification exam.

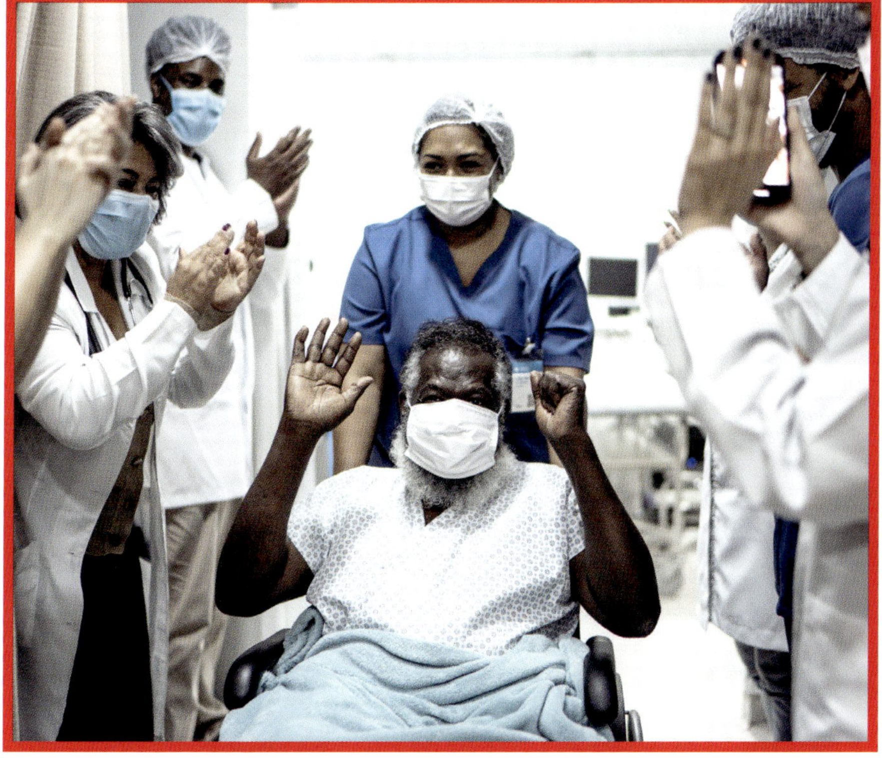

Nurses play an important role in supporting and cheering on their patients.

Another career pathway is as an orderly. Orderlies help in transferring patients and cleaning and stocking medical equipment and facilities. They need to have a high school diploma and on-the-job training. Nursing assistants and orderlies make an average of $38,000 a year.

Home Health and Personal Care Aides

Home health aides and personal care aides give basic care to individual patients in their homes. Home health aides typically work under the supervision of nurses or other medical staff. They help patients with their daily care needs. In some states, they are also able to provide basic medical care for patients such as checking vital signs, giving medications, or helping with wound or skin care. Personal care aides generally only provide nonmedical care such as assistance with cooking, cleaning, and transportation. These careers typically require a high school diploma. Depending on the state that they work in, aides may be required to take a test to obtain a license or certification. Home health aides and personal care aides make an average of $33,500 a year.

Additional Health-Care Career Pathways

Most people are generally familiar with what a career as a physician or nurse entails. But there are many more career opportunities for people interested in patient care. Many of these additional career options require less extensive postsecondary education than that of a physician.

Medical Assistants

Medical assistants help with clinical and administrative medical tasks. They can record patient medical histories, perform basic tests, and assist with preparing and cleaning medical supplies and instruments. Medical assistants typically have to complete a postsecondary certificate program or an associate's degree. They make an average of $42,000 a year.

Home health aides provide care in the comfort of a patient's home.

Additional Health-Care Careers

The health-care field has so many different career opportunities that we couldn't possibly go into detail about them all in this book. Here are some other career opportunities that might be appealing if you have the desire to help others.

Therapists

Therapists treat and assist in rehabilitating patients who are suffering from injury or disease. They typically focus on helping patients without the use of medicine or surgery. There are many types of therapists. Physical therapists help people struggling with physical injuries or illnesses. They help people manage their pain and increase their mobility. Occupational therapists help patients create and maintain skills they need to succeed in living and working independently. They often help people with long-term disabilities or conditions better manage their daily tasks and quality of life. Recreational therapists use music, art, sports, and other engaging activities to help enhance the emotional and physical well-being of patients. Respiratory therapists assist patients who have trouble breathing from diseases such as asthma. Mental health therapists treat and counsel patients who have a wide variety of emotional, behavioral, or mental health concerns. These therapists can work with individuals, couples, or entire families to help people enhance their well-being and coping strategies.

Dentists

Dentists focus on the health of a patient's teeth, mouth, and jaw. Dental hygienists and dental assistants help them.

Optometrists

Optometrists focus on the health of a patient's eyes. They often work alongside opticians, who help fit patients for glasses and contacts.

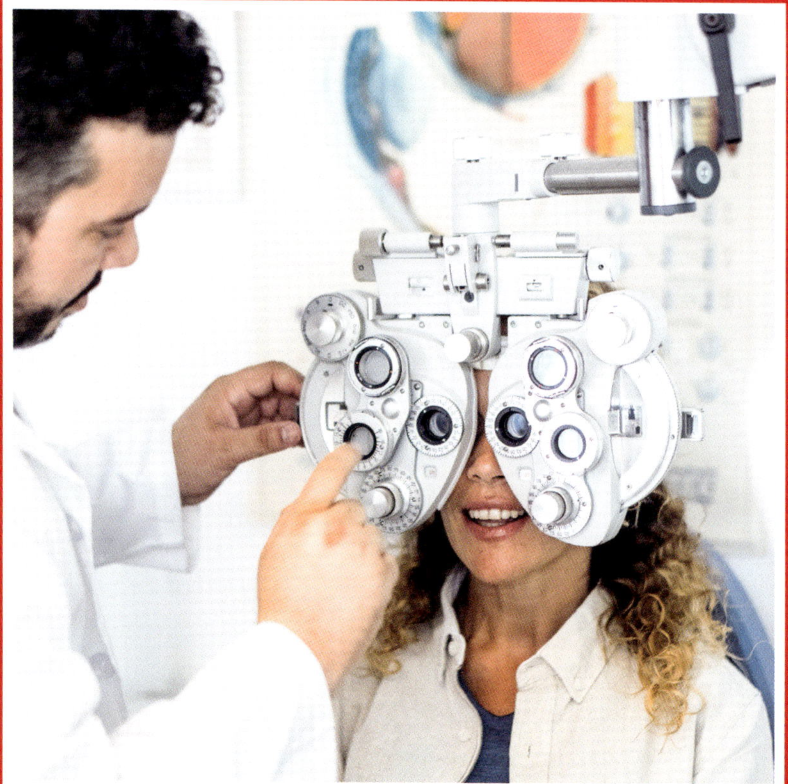

Optometrists provide patients with vision care and help them choose the necessary eyewear to ensure that they see the world around them clearly.

Pharmacists

Pharmacists fill medication prescriptions for customers. They also answer questions and provide information for patients about medicine. Pharmacy technicians assist them.

Dietitians and Nutritionists

Dietitians and nutritionists use their knowledge of nutrition to help patients manage illness and their dietary needs.

Medical Records Specialists

Medical records specialists are in charge of compiling and managing patient records. They oversee data entry and recordkeeping. Medical records specialists have a variety of educational paths they can follow. Some have a high school diploma while others have a college degree. Regardless, pursuing a certification program can be beneficial in finding employment. Medical records specialists make an average of $49,000 a year.

Paramedics and Emergency Medical Technicians

Paramedics and emergency medical technicians (EMTs) assist patients in emergency scenarios. They are often also in charge of transporting patients to a hospital in an ambulance or helicopter during an emergency. EMTs and paramedics require slightly different levels of education. Most EMTs need to complete a basic certification course that usually takes less than a year to complete. While you typically need to be eighteen years old, younger high school students are able to pursue EMT certification in some states. Paramedics first need EMT certification before they complete additional education requirements. EMTs make an average of $39,000 a year while paramedics earn approximately $53,000 a year.

Phlebotomists

Phlebotomists are in charge of drawing blood from patients and preparing it for testing or donation. They work in hospitals, clinics, or blood donation centers. Most phlebotomists have completed a postsecondary educational program that lasts less than a year. They make about $42,000 a year.

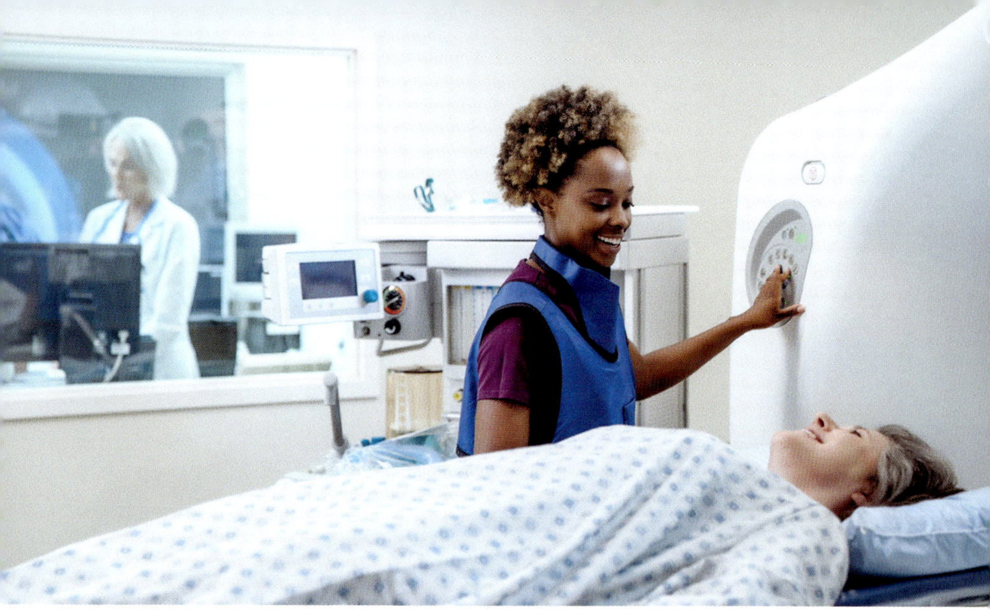

Technicians help prepare patients for a variety of imaging scans.

Radiologic and MRI Technologists

Radiologic technologists perform X-rays and additional imaging for patients. Magnetic resonance imaging (MRI) technologists perform a similar role in managing and operating MRI machines. Most technologist positions require an associate's degree. They make an average of $76,000.

Sonographers and Cardiovascular Technologists

Sonographers and cardiovascular technologists oversee additional imaging and testing for patients. Sonographers perform ultrasounds, or imaging of a body's organs and tissues. Cardiovascular technologists perform tests such as an electrocardiogram, more commonly called an EKG, specifically on a patient's heart and lungs. Sonographers and cardiovascular technologists typically need an associate's degree or to go through a postsecondary certificate program. Sonographers make $84,470 a year, while cardiovascular technologists make $66,170.

CHAPTER THREE

A Day in the Life

Depending on a person's specific job, there is typically a lot of variety in the day-to-day work of a health-care professional. Working with different patients and different conditions often helps make every day unique.

When choosing a career, it is important to look at the work environment and schedule and think about how that career could fit in with your desired lifestyle. Do you like having a lot of variety in your work? Do you prefer to have a standard work schedule? Do you prefer a fast-paced or a slower environment? Health-care careers in particular often have demanding schedules. Let's dig a little deeper into what life is like as a health-care worker.

Work Environments

Most health-care professionals work inside a variety of medical facilities. Some positions allow people to spend their time in multiple types of facilities. For example, physicians often see their patients in a private clinic and also take

Every workday is unique for health-care providers.

rotating shifts visiting patients or performing surgery in a hospital setting. Many other job positions are needed in a variety of facilities. Nurses, for example, work at hospitals, clinics, and residential care facilities. However, their roles, responsibilities, and schedules can vary greatly depending on the location where they work.

Hospitals

Many health-care positions are based in hospital settings. Hospitals are typically large and employ a lot of different people and professions. Hospitals work with patients who have more serious needs. Many patients will end up staying in a hospital overnight or for several days. Other patients visit hospitals for emergency services.

Hospitals serve a large variety of patients and health needs. They tend to be in larger towns and cities. People who live in rural areas may have to travel significant distances to get to a hospital. In certain cases, if a patient needs specialized emergency care, they may need to be medically transported to a larger hospital that has the resources to best assist them.

In larger urban areas, some hospitals may specialize in services to special populations such as pediatric patients or military veterans. Emergency health-care needs never take a holiday, and neither do hospitals. Hospitals stay open at all hours every day of the year.

Clinics

Medical clinics offer a wide variety of generalized and specialty care to patients. Clinics offer nonemergency care to patients, and they are typically much smaller than hospitals. Many clinics offer preventative or routine care, and patients

EMTs transport patients from their home or the scene of an accident to the hospital, or between health-care settings.

usually make an appointment in advance. Other clinics offer specialized services for almost any nonemergency medical need. It is common for patients to visit a clinic for a doctor's appointment and then schedule surgery that happens at a hospital or a surgery center.

Unlike hospitals, clinics are not always open. They usually keep more standard weekday hours, open from approximately eight o'clock in the morning until five o'clock in the evening. Some clinics also offer limited weekend hours.

In certain communities, mobile clinics are also an option. Mobile clinics are not in established buildings. Instead, they are small clinics based in vans or other vehicles. Most mobile clinics provide preventative health-care services such as basic exams, screenings, vaccinations, or health education. Mobile clinics serve rural and other underserved communities and populations.

Residential Care Facilities

There are many different types of residential care facilities. These are facilities where patients who need daily care and support live long-term. Nursing homes, rehabilitation centers, and group homes are all examples of patient housing facilities that employ health-care workers. Like hospitals, care facilities are always open, and patients need care around the clock. Patients often need assistance with daily needs such as eating, transportation, and personal hygiene. Many facilities also provide basic medical care and therapeutic services that help patients manage chronic conditions.

In-Home Patient Care

In some cases, patients with specific needs or chronic conditions may qualify for in-home care. Depending on the extent of a patient's needs, a health-care worker may work full-time with one patient. Other times, a health-care worker may travel between private homes and assist multiple patients in a day. Most in-home health-care workers are either home health aides or personal care aides.

Work Schedule

Health care doesn't take a day off. Illnesses and injuries occur at all times. Thinking about your preferred work schedule is an important part of choosing a health-care career and job position that is best for you. Most hospital and residential care

Many patients benefit from being able to live at home while receiving additional care.

Health Care on the Go

A career in the health-care field may not be the first thing that comes to mind if you are looking for a sense of adventure. But don't overlook this option. Many health-care careers still offer opportunities for travel. While the majority of health-care professionals work inside a hospital or clinic, there are some exceptions. EMTs and paramedics, for example, are often on the move in their local areas as they work in the field transporting patients. But there are other opportunities to pursue health care on the road.

Military

The military requires and employs a wide variety of health-care professionals. Most of the same jobs and skill sets that are required in traditional health-care work are also necessary and beneficial in the military. If you are interested in a career in the military, it might be worth looking into what opportunities they offer to help support your education.

Traveling Positions

Some health-care positions are in such high demand that travel opportunities are often available. Travel nursing, for example, helps bring additional nurses to communities that have a high need for them. Traveling positions are usually temporary positions. They often offer highly competitive pay and additional perks such as housing stipends to attract potential employees.

Volunteering Positions

Some health-care organizations also offer volunteer opportunities. Doctors Without Borders, also known as Médecins Sans Frontières, provides medical care internationally in underserved areas, locations affected by natural disasters, and conflict zones. But you don't have to go abroad to find

locations that could use additional help. Local events such as music festivals or marathons are often looking for volunteers to help keep participants safe. If you are interested in helping in areas that are in the greatest need for health-care assistance, then volunteering might be an enriching opportunity.

Practicing proper handwashing techniques is an important part of hygiene as a health-care worker.

facility employees work in shifts. Common shifts last eight hours on a day, evening, or night shift. Other employees often work twelve-hour shifts either during the day or at night.

Because health-care situations can be unpredictable, many jobs also have "on call" hours. Employees who are on call need to be ready to report to work immediately if they are needed regardless of the time of day.

When choosing a job in health care, it's helpful to understand the typical schedule. In addition to potentially long shifts or on-call hours, many jobs also require working evenings, weekends, and even holidays. Finding how to balance your work life with your personal life is an important skill for most health-care workers.

Work Challenges

Health-care workers face a variety of physical challenges in their line of work. Most health-care professionals have physically active jobs that require a lot of standing, walking, bending, and moving. Many nursing professionals need to be particularly careful to avoid back injuries while lifting, moving, and transferring patients.

Health-care workers must be mindful to stay healthy. They often come in close contact with both patients and bodily fluids that may spread infectious diseases. It is important that workers take steps to protect their health by wearing personal protective equipment (PPE), maintaining handwashing procedures, and following the safety procedures at their jobs. This challenge became extremely clear throughout the COVID-19 pandemic. Health-care workers put their own health and lives at risk to assist others in a time of emergency.

Not as Seen on TV

For decades, medical television dramas have captured the attention of casual fans and aspiring future health-care providers alike. These medical TV shows are fast-paced, dramatic, and entertaining. But they aren't always accurate. While they are fun to watch, if a thrilling episode of *Grey's Anatomy* inspired you to pursue a health-care career, just make sure you have the real facts first.

One of the biggest differences between TV and real life is the level of drama involved. Most TV shows focus on emergency medicine, and they depict health care as fast-paced and dramatic. While that can be the case, in reality, health care can also often be more mundane and repetitive. After all, filling out paperwork and drawing the twentieth vial of blood of the day are important tasks, but they don't really make thrilling television. Medical dramas also tend to focus on physicians, and there is less representation of other health-care careers in non-hospital environments.

Regardless of their accuracy, TV shows do influence viewers' perceptions of what a career in health care is like. In an article about a research study that showed one important difference between TV and real life, author Alyssa Malmquist explained, "For example, when patients receive cardiopulmonary resuscitation (CPR) on these shows, they're revived about 75% of the time. That's 10 times higher than real-life survival rates, which means viewers may have a perception that CPR is more effective than it is in reality."

You don't have to put down the remote just yet, but make sure that you think critically about what you see on TV!

Health-care professionals wear PPE to protect themselves while doing their jobs. PPE includes, but is not limited to, surgical masks, goggles, disposable gloves, caps, and paper gowns.

Many employees also run the risk of coming into contact with harmful substances. Phlebotomists and nurses must be careful to avoid an accidental needle stick. Radiation technologists need to take caution to minimize their exposure to dangerous radiation from X-ray machines.

CHAPTER FOUR

How to Pursue Your Health-Care Dreams

Each specific career in health care necessitates a different education. There are many jobs that only require a high school diploma. A number of other careers require a certificate program after high school. Other options require a college degree or even additional advanced degrees, such as a master's or doctorate. There are a wide variety of options no matter how much schooling you want to pursue.

Regardless of how much future education you are planning on, if you are passionate about a future in health care, you don't have to wait to start preparing. Almost every high school offers plenty of courses that will come in handy as you build your knowledge. Obviously, any courses that directly teach about medicine or health care are a good idea to prepare you for your next step. Some high schools offer opportunities for certification in health-care skills, including first aid, CPR, or even EMT certification. These are great opportunities to take advantage of if they are available at your school or in your community. But there are other courses and extracurricular opportunities that will help prepare you for a

Students often practice learning new skills on medical manikins.

career in health care. Don't be afraid to think outside the box. Future health-care providers can learn a lot from all sorts of different subjects.

Science

Almost all health-care careers require a strong background in science. In particular, courses in anatomy, physiology, biology, and chemistry are helpful in preparing students for the knowledge they will need either in college or on the job. Having a strong understanding of the scientific process and the workings of the human body are essential skills for almost any health-care professional.

Math

Health care couldn't exist without math. Math is essential to helping understand vital signs and determining appropriate treatments and effective, safe levels of medicine for patients. Most health-care workers need a solid background in math.

English and Communications

Health-care professionals have to be clear communicators in order to communicate with colleagues and patients. Learning to effectively communicate and becoming a comfortable public speaker will assist you in your career. Honing your written communication is also beneficial. Successful health-care providers need to provide clear and concise written instructions and visit notes to their patients.

A solid foundation in math is necessary in most health-care positions.

Social Studies

Health-care workers don't only need to have knowledge of the human body. It is also important for them to understand and appreciate the social, emotional, mental, and cultural needs of patients. Patients are whole people, not just a list of symptoms. Many people and communities have beliefs about their health and wellness that medical professionals must understand and respect. Courses in psychology and sociology in particular are helpful in learning how to treat people holistically.

Technology

Most health-care providers frequently use computers and advanced machinery in their work. Having a basic understanding of technology will be beneficial for health-care workers.

Volunteering is a great way to give back to your community and practice important caregiving skills.

Extracurricular Opportunities

Coursework is an important place to start as you prepare for a career in health care. However, there are also plenty of opportunities to get involved and learn more outside of a traditional classroom. After all, studying human anatomy is beneficial, but you can't learn how to successfully draw blood from a book. Some medical skills can only come from hands-on, repetitive practice.

Jobs and Volunteering

One of the primary ways to learn more about health care is to start working or volunteering in the field. Of course, you aren't going to be performing surgery in high school, but there are a number of ways that you can get involved in the health-care field as early as the age of sixteen. A few jobs, such as nursing assistants and EMTs, are occasionally available to students in high school. These are fantastic opportunities to begin your career caring for patients. But even if you can't get a job that involves direct patient care, volunteering in a health-care facility can be a great alternative.

Many hospitals and nursing homes are often looking for volunteers. Typical hospital volunteer duties include restocking supplies, staffing information desks, helping transport patients, or working in the hospital gift shop. Nursing homes and other residential care facilities are happy to have volunteers who can spend time with patients and provide enrichment activities. It can often be lonely for patients to be away from their families and living in a residential care setting. Volunteers who play music, lead craft activities, or even call bingo numbers can go a long way in

More Hands-On Learning: Job Shadowing

While reading about and researching health-care careers is a good start, one of the best ways to learn more is to see what these jobs are like for yourself. Maybe a career as a phlebotomist sounds like fun until you try it and realize that you can't stand the sight of blood! Getting a hands-on understanding of what a particular job entails before you invest your time and education in that pathway can be helpful. And one of the best ways to truly understand a career is to participate in job shadowing. Job shadowing is when you follow a professional at their work to see what their job is really like on a daily basis. You can witness what a typical day is like, how they interact with patients, and what the upsides and challenges of the career are. This can be especially helpful for health-care careers that have very specific requirements.

Many health-care providers are happy to share information about their career path with interested young people. Try tapping into your network to see if anyone knows someone who would be willing to allow you to shadow them for a day. Think about your family, neighbors, and the family of your friends. Is there anyone who works in health care? Don't forget to reach out to the health-care professionals you already know. Start with the doctors and nurses who have helped treat you in the past. Consider reaching out to local clinics or hospitals and ask if they have any shadowing opportunities for high school students. There are even some programs that offer virtual job shadowing opportunities.

So get out there and give it a try. You might even learn something that surprises you as you start to narrow down your career options.

Many high schools and community colleges offer hands-on learning experiences for students interested in pursuing nursing or another health-care career. Students work with professionals in the field to learn basic techniques and safety practices.

making a patient's day a little brighter. All these volunteer opportunities are also helpful in building your patient care skill set. The more time and opportunities you have working with patients and their families, the better prepared you will be for your eventual career.

CHAPTER FIVE

The Future of Health-Care Careers

The need for health care is growing quickly as the population grows and ages. People will always continue to need health-care services. The Occupational Outlook Handbook maintained by the US Bureau of Labor Statistics predicts that there will be about 1.9 million job openings in the health-care field every year. The overall demand for health-care workers who diagnose and treat patients is set to grow 9 percent between 2023 and 2033. This is higher than the average job growth rate of 3 percent.

There are a few careers that have especially high demand and huge growth opportunities. Nurse practitioner positions are projected to grow by 40 percent in that decade. Physician assistant roles are anticipated to grow by 28 percent. Both these career paths require an advanced degree beyond a bachelor's degree. There are other career paths that require less advanced education but are still projected to have huge growth too. Medical assistant roles are predicted to grow by 15 percent, while home health and personal care aides are predicted to have a 21 percent growth. Regardless of what specific health-care career you are interested in, chances are good that there will continue to be demand and growth in the field.

The health-care field grows constantly. Physicians, nurses, and other health-care professionals are always in high demand.

New Trends in Health Care

In addition to growing quickly, health care is also always changing. This is part of what makes these jobs so appealing for some people. An important part of a health-care worker's job is to stay up-to-date on the technology trends and changes in the field.

Telehealth Services

As computer technology and virtual communication options have expanded, they have become increasingly important in health care. Telehealth, also known as telemedicine, provides health care to patients remotely through video, phone, and chat communications. Telehealth has been growing in popularity in the 2020s, especially since the start of the COVID-19 pandemic. In 2022 approximately 25 percent of patients used telehealth services. That is much higher than the only 5 percent of patients who utilized telehealth before COVID-19 but significantly lower than it was at the very height of the pandemic in 2020 when 70 percent of patients utilized the option.

There are a number of benefits of telehealth for both patients and health-care providers. Telehealth has allowed health-care providers the ability to reach more patients, especially those who live in rural areas with fewer medical care options available. It is also a helpful and convenient option for patients who may find it challenging to leave their homes. Getting a telehealth appointment can often be faster and more convenient for patients. Telehealth also gives health-care providers the opportunity to work remotely or from home. This can give them more flexibility and

New technologies and telehealth services impact the way people access health care.

increase safety and health for workers, as they are exposed to infectious diseases less.

But there are some downsides of telehealth. Not every type of medical appointment can be done virtually. Telehealth isn't an option for some health-care professions that need to have physical access to a patient to do testing. Plus, the majority of patients and health-care providers still prefer the traditional in-person appointment model that includes a comprehensive physical examination.

Taking Care of Yourself While Taking Care of Others

Careers in health care are often challenging. Heavy workloads, intense schedules, emotionally challenging situations, and a lack of support often lead to work stress. Stress among health-care workers has become more severe since the start of the COVID-19 pandemic.

The challenges that health-care workers face sometimes lead to burnout. Career burnout happens when job stress becomes too overwhelming, and employees quit their jobs or even change careers entirely. Burnout in health-care fields can lead to worker shortages. These shortages can then place even more stress on people still working in the health-care field.

However, there are things that everyone can do to help reduce health-care worker stress and burnout. The US Department of Health and Human Services has created a list of recommendations for health-care workers to help manage stress and reduce burnout.

Look Out for Signs of Burnout

The first step in taking care of yourself and your colleagues is to learn about what burnout looks like. Major signs of distress and burnout include exhaustion, a feeling of being emotionally unavailable or lacking compassion that you used to have, and beginning to doubt whether your work is meaningful or worthwhile. Keeping an eye out for signs of burnout in yourself and in others may help you seek change before it becomes too severe.

Stay Connected

Staying connected and reaching out for help are important steps in combating burnout. Remember that you aren't alone in career stress. Lean on your coworkers for support and make sure to offer support in return. Look for opportunities in your workplace to take care of your mental health and prioritize teamwork and support.

Prioritize Joy

Work life, especially in health care, can often take up a lot of time and energy. But don't forget to prioritize time for joy in your life. Enjoy hobbies and relaxing time with your friends, family, and coworkers. Look for joy both in your work and outside of work. Connecting with others and looking for small positive moments in your day helps you manage stress and find better life balance.

Take Care of Yourself

Health-care workers prioritize the health and well-being of others. But that doesn't mean that you should neglect your own health. Get enough sleep, eat nourishing foods, and find time to exercise. Taking care of yourself will also help set a good example for patients and make sure that you have the stamina to keep up with the physical demands of your job.

Advocate for Change

Stress and burnout can be very challenging. But these challenges also give you the opportunity to advocate for changes to your workplace. Look for positive changes that you can help create and use your voice to make work a more positive place for everyone.

There are also ways to help support health-care workers before you are one. It is never too early to reach out and offer your support to these professionals. Don't underestimate the importance of kindness. One of the best ways to support health-care workers is to simply be kind when you are a patient in a health-care situation.

Artificial Intelligence in Health Care

Artificial intelligence (AI) is influencing many different career paths, and the field of health care is no exception. In fact, there are many interesting and exciting ways that AI can benefit health-care providers. Many providers are using AI to help save time. Staying up-to-date on the newest research can be very time-consuming, but AI can help. As the Mayo Clinic explains, "AI can work with huge volumes of information—from medical journals to healthcare records—and highlight the most relevant pieces." AI is also being used to help analyze diagnostic tests and predict disease.

A researcher uses virtual reality to experiment with new treatment methods. Virtual reality and AI open up new possibilities for what the future of health care may look like.

However, there are also some downsides and potential concerns about the impact of AI. Health-care providers are trusted to give equal and quality care to all patients regardless of their background. But research has shown that health-care providers, whether they realize it or not, often demonstrate implicit bias on the basis of race, ethnicity, gender, socioeconomic status, religion, disability, or sexual orientation. As explained in a *Medical News Today* article, "Bias and discrimination occur at both the interpersonal and the institutional level of healthcare. Bias can lead to people receiving poor treatment, receiving inaccurate diagnoses, or experiencing delays in diagnosis."

Bias in health care is no longer a uniquely human problem. AI does not create wholly new information. Instead, AI excels at analyzing large amounts of data and making conclusions based on that data. But AI is only as good as the data that it analyzes. Since AI uses data that has human bias, it can lead to continuing and spreading bias in health care if it isn't trained properly.

Some people are worried that AI will take over human jobs. Other experts disagree. They caution that jobs aren't going to be lost to AI, but that they will simply change and evolve. AI is a powerful tool. But at the end of the day, it is just a tool that needs a person to run it. And while it can help health-care providers, it still needs well-trained people to run and use it. In fact, the American Medical Association often refers to AI as augmented intelligence.

CONCLUSION

A Passion for Care

Health care is a growing field that will always have a variety of jobs available. While a career in health care can be challenging with long hours and demanding work, it is also very rewarding for many people. Health-care workers can make an impact on people's lives. They have the power to heal, care, and inspire. That power also requires a tremendous amount of responsibility. Health-care workers need to tap into their maturity, empathy, and wisdom to help improve lives.

In order to succeed in a demanding field, it's important to care about your line of work. Think about what is drawing you toward a career in the medical field. Are you passionate about helping people heal? Are you curious and always want to be learning more throughout your career? Do you love educating patients about how to maintain their own health and well-being? Try making a list of what is most important to you in a health-care career. Having a set of core values supporting your career path will help you to stay motivated and excited, even on your challenging days. All jobs have their ups and downs, but having passion for what you do helps make it all worth it.

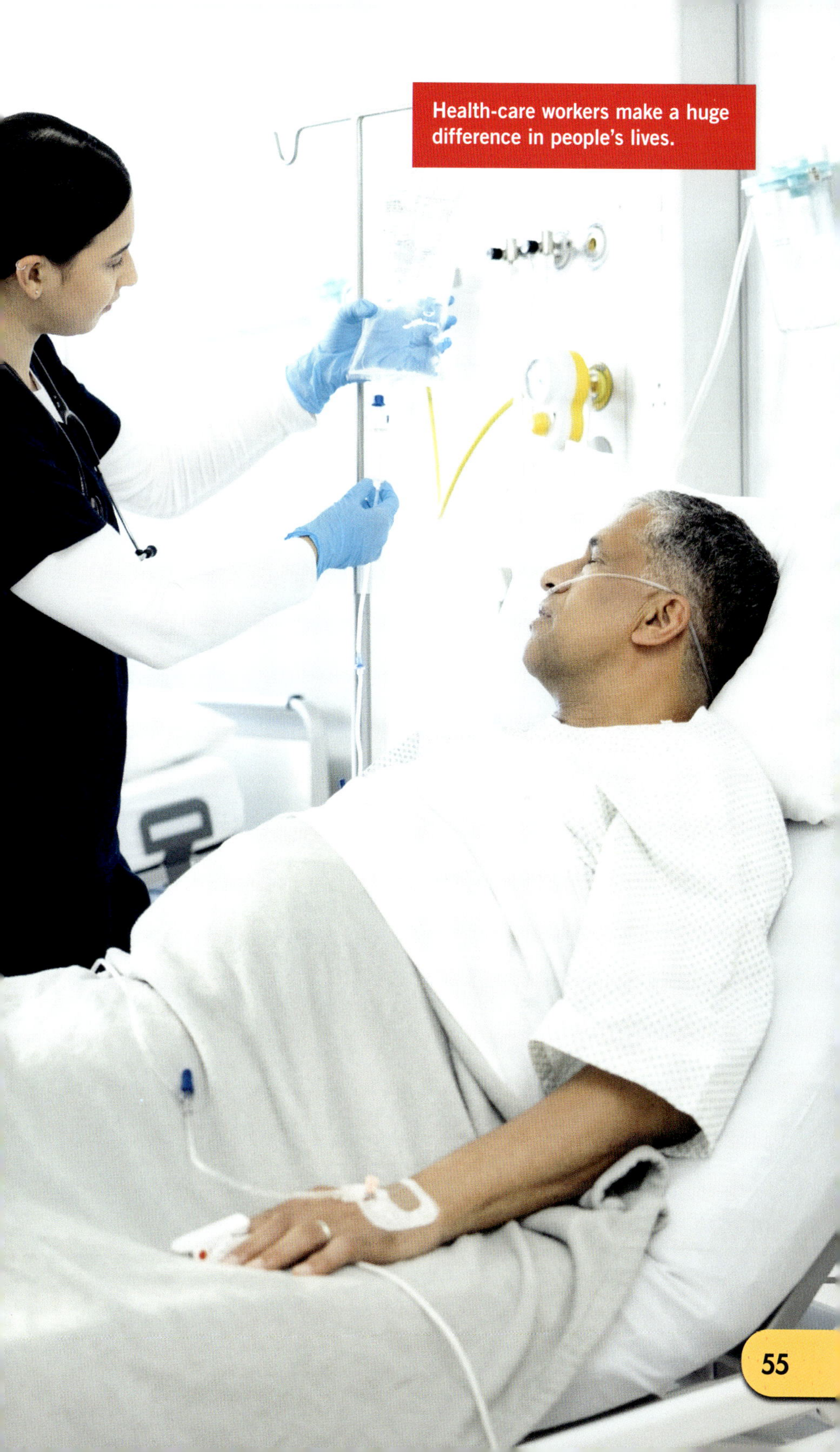

Health-care workers make a huge difference in people's lives.

GLOSSARY

bias: a personal judgment or prejudice

burnout: exhaustion as a result of prolonged stress

chronic: an illness that is ongoing or occurs again and again

colleague: a coworker or professional one works with

compassion: sympathy for others' suffering and a desire to help

competent: having the necessary ability, knowledge, or skill

determination: the act of making a firm decision

diagnosis: the act of identifying a disease based on symptoms

discretion: the quality of being cautious or discreet in what one says

efficiency: the quality of producing positive results without wasting time or energy

facility: a building established for a specific purpose

geriatric: a branch of medicine that focuses on elder adults

hierarchy: an arrangement of people into ranks or classes

holistic: treatment that focuses on both the body and mind

hygiene: practices that help maintain health and cleanliness

infectious: a disease that is capable of being spread to others

integrity: the quality of being honest and sincere

manipulation: to adjust or move something by hand

neurology: a branch of medicine that focuses on the brain

personal protective equipment (PPE): items such as gloves, masks, and gowns that help protect workers

postsecondary: education after and beyond high school

preventative: concerned with preventing or keeping something from happening

radiation: energy given off in waves or particles, often from X-ray machines

rehabilitating: fixing or restoring to a former state

resilience: the ability to recover or adjust to change

revived: returned to consciousness or life

specialize: focus on one specific area

stipends: money paid to offset living expenses

therapeutic: using healing methods to help treat diseases or disorders

vital signs: indications of life such as one's pulse, temperature, or blood pressure

SOURCE NOTES

10 "According to research . . . of health care.": Ted A. James, "Teamwork as a Core Value in Heath Care," Harvard Medical School, August 6, 2021, https://postgraduateeducation.hms.harvard.edu/trends-medicine/teamwork-core-value-health-care.

36 "For example, when . . . is in reality.": Alyssa Malmquist, "Here's What to Know About the Accuracy of TV Medical Shows," Mass General Brigham Health Plan, December 28, 2022, https://blog.massgeneralbrighamhealthplan.org/heres-what-to-know-about-the-accuracy-of-tv-medical-shows.

52 "AI can work . . . most relevant pieces.": Mayo Clinic Press Editors, "AI in Healthcare: The Future of Patient Care and Health Management," *Mayo Clinic Press*, March 27, 2024, https://mcpress.mayoclinic.org/healthy-aging/ai-in-healthcare-the-future-of-patient-care-and-health-management/.

53 "Bias and discrimination . . . delays in diagnosis.": Anna Smith Haghighi, "Biases in Healthcare: An Overview," *Medical News Today*, updated August 23, 2023, https://www.medicalnewstoday.com/articles/biases-in-healthcare.

SELECTED BIBLIOGRAPHY

Greiner, Ann, and Elisa Knebel, eds. *Health Professions Education: A Bridge to Quality*. Washington, DC: National Academies Press, 2023.

Haghighi, Anna Smith. "Biases in Healthcare: An Overview." *Medical News Today*. Updated August 23, 2023. https://www.medicalnewstoday.com/articles/biases-in-healthcare.

"Health Worker Burnout." US Department of Health and Human Services. Updated August 2, 2024. https://www.hhs.gov/surgeongeneral/priorities/health-worker-burnout/index.html.

"Healthcare Occupations." Occupational Outlook Handbook. Updated August 29, 2024. https://www.bls.gov/ooh/healthcare/home.htm.

James, Ted A. "Teamwork as a Core Value in Health Care." Harvard Medical School, August 6, 2021. https://postgraduateeducation.hms.harvard.edu/trends-medicine/teamwork-core-value-health-care.

Mayo Clinic Press Editors. "AI in Healthcare: The Future of Patient Care and Health Management." *Mayo Clinic Press*, March 7, 2024. https://mcpress.mayoclinic.org/healthy-aging/ai-in-healthcare-the-future-of-patient-care-and-health-management/.

FURTHER INFORMATION

Books

Barth, Kelley. *Exploring Service Trades Careers.* Minneapolis: Twenty-First Century Books: 2026.
Health-care professionals provide medical services to people. Many other jobs focus on service too. This guide covers careers in hospitality, food service, and more.

Cartlidge, Cherese. *Skilled Jobs in Health Care.* San Diego: ReferencePoint, 2021.
Cartlidge provides an overview of a variety of career options in the health-care industry.

Hunter, Nick. *Artificial Intelligence in Healthcare: Will AI Help Us or Hurt Us?* Shropshire, UK: Cheriton Children's Books, 2024.
This book explores the pros and cons of how artificial intelligence will impact the future of health care.

Scientific American Editors. *The Future of Medicine.* 1st ed. New York: Scientific American Educational Publishing, 2024.
Scientific American discusses how technology is continuing to change and evolve the field of health care.

Small, Cathleen. *How to Choose Your Perfect Healthcare Career.* Shropshire, UK: Cheriton Children's Books, 2023.
Unique personality tests help readers learn about what type of health-care career path may be a good fit for them.

Websites

Adolescent and School Health

https://www.cdc.gov/HealthyYouth/

The Centers for Disease Control and Prevention provide helpful information about health topics that most commonly impact teens.

ExploreHealthCareers.org

https://explorehealthcareers.org/

This site offers detailed information about different health-care careers and tips for how to prepare for them.

Explore Healthcare Careers

https://college.mayo.edu/academics/explore-health-care-careers/

Mayo Clinic shares a comprehensive overview of different health-care careers

Health Worker Burnout

https://www.hhs.gov/surgeongeneral/priorities/health-worker-burnout/index.html

The US Department of Heath and Human services offers helpful information about recognizing and avoiding burnout in health-care careers at this page.

HOSA: Future Health Professionals

https://hosa.org/

HOSA is an organization that provides resources to help prepare and encourage future health professionals.

INDEX

ABOUT THE AUTHOR

Kelley Barth is a former children's librarian who loves connecting with young people over stories and books. When she isn't busy writing, she enjoys reading, hiking, crafting, and going on adventures with her husband and son.

PHOTO ACKNOWLEDGMENTS

Image credits: FatCamera/E+/Getty Images, p. 5; Sean Anthony Eddy/E+/Getty Images, p.7; sturti/E+/Getty Images, p. 9; Tom Werner/DigitalVision/Getty Images, p. 11; FatCamera/E+/Getty Images, p. 12; Sam Edwards/OJO Images/Getty Images, p. 15; Heath Korvola/DigitalVision/Getty Images, p. 16; FG Trade/E+/Getty Images, p. 19; FG Trade/E+/Getty Images, p. 21; Westend61/Westend61/Getty Images, p. 23; FS Productions/Tetra images/Getty Images, p. 25; Reza Estakhrian/The Image Bank/Getty Images, p. 27; JazzzIRT/E+/Getty Images, p. 29; MoMo Productions/DigitalVision/Getty Images, p. 31; Courtney Hale/E+/Getty Images, p. 33; Stígur Már Karlsson/Heimsmyndir/E+/Getty Images, p 34; Morsa Images/E+/Getty Images, p. 37; Ariel Shelley/Digital Vision/Getty Images, p. 39; Alex Walker/Moment/Getty Images, p. 41; sturti/E+/Getty Images, p. 42; martindoucet/E+/Getty Images, p. 45; mixetto/E+/Getty Images, p. 47; AJ_Watt/E+/Getty Images, p. 49; Moyo Studio/E+/Getty Images, p. 52; Kobus Louw/E+/Getty Images, p. 55.

Cover image: andreser/E+/Getty Images